HUMANS :

A STUDY

by

Rachel Aston Warren

Warren, Rachel Aston
1st edition.
ISBN: 978-0692695616
Prolegomenon Publishing

Edited by Jenn Storey
Cover Developed by Nai Obeid
Front Cover Photo by Rachel Aston Warren
Back Cover Manipulated by Jenn Storey
Author Photo by Jenn Storey

Composed and released in Austin, TX

raw_artistry@yahoo.com

2

Humans: A Study *is a psychological study on humans, depicted through poetry and prose. It is a linguistic photograph of human life on Earth, middle America; of connections had, or almost had. The study intends to start a conversation on universal experiences, welcoming inquiry, doubt, and compassionate support. Though it does not answer every question it asks, it tackles very real topics including mental health, friendship, possession, and inevitably, death.* Humans: A Study *proves not why we exist, but only, certainly, that we exist.*

TABLE OF CONTENTS

BACKGROUND

WE SAT ON THE FLOOR A LOT

We sat on the floor a lot,
You and I.

It was our peace field
Our mediation arena
Our restart mat

It brought us back to the ground.
To each other
Allowing us to be open.

It was our communication creek
Our gameless zone
Our humbling code

We sat on the floor a lot,
You and I.

I need that again.
Please, love
Come sit on the floor with me.

PROST

For when you watched her, looking at her own, self
Eye-lids half-mast, putting on the make-up

When she said You ever have the days you wanna look like a ghost?

To the half-hearted, the peripheried, the mostly melancholy

For when your eyelids were lead, couldn't get out of bed
They made you breakfast, coffee, a french lesson

When you walked home she was on the lawn in her pajamas pushing a
stroller back and forth over the grass as if it were not a stroller but a
lawnmower only it was a stroller and the stroller was empty

To the well-intentioned, the resourceful, the lost

For when the sun made a half-moon of your eye-lids
And the underground humidity got you high

When the infant next door had four equal teachers but they don't know yet it
made him deaf

To being raised by a village, a textbook, a lamp-post
Prost

22

How badly I wanted to be back in that time-
That simple time-
When the highlight of my summer was the night my dad made popcorn on the stove
And we sat on the porch reading quietly, independently.
The popcorn pot on a burned and stained potholder hot in my lap.
Just breezy enough to be wearing shorts and a crewneck Winnie The Pooh sweatshirt.

The only thing keeping time, the cicadas' drone of mid-August:
The drone, the mating call, the hymn, the sob.
I've always wanted a sound machine to play cicada tears
To lull me back to a time where I danced to them.
Where the fireflies felt the beat,
And the firecrackers had their cause,
And everything else was still.

The time when I didn't feel the choke of guilt for spacing out for hours to the soothing sounds of bug sex.

CONTENTLESS SCENE

A: How do you know?

B: They told me.

A: Really?

B: Really. How do you?

A: I just know.

B: Sure.

A: So what should we do?

B: Celebrate?

A: That's your call.

BECAUSE

Because that stranger wasn't afraid to make teary-eyed contact
And ask if I was going to be okay
Or maybe he told me so
I can't remember anymore
Either way
It was so much better than
Happy Birthday

LEMONGRASS

Remember when parents and teachers used to say
It's supposed to sting
If it hurts that means it's healing

FADING

We were falling asleep.
He was on top of me,
I was thinking of him.
I was imagining, asking him, questioning him:
"Who are you?"

In my mind, he stared
On top of me, he snored.

I asked him again,
"Who are you?"
I turned internally unto myself;
Asked myself, questioned myself:
"Who am I?"

Just as I posed it, he jolted awake
And, scared, quickly said,
"Am I?"

WHO AM I?

I am disinterested and I am in love
I am a grinning, fading, celestial body
I am half bitter, half naked
I am always with you
And I am a liar
What am I?

WE WILL DROWN IN RAGE IF WE'RE NOT CAREFUL

Napped, nibbled, trimmed, ignored, scrolled, erased, lathered, created,
browsed, denied
Call it self-care
Laid, lied, hiccuped, squinted, interrupted, spilled, guessed, chuckled,
stubbed, forgave
Call it God
Stroked, swayed, drenched, characterized, skipped, cried, introduced,
fornicated, decorated, left
Call it whatever the fuck you want

THE TOKEN

The girl in the green dress walked up to the row of tables, found the only empty one, and sat down on the uneven chair as if the back might burn her. She looked out at the parking lot like she was trying to read it; the crease in her brow mirroring that of her breasts, pushed up and in ever so slightly. Her feet were still, her hands securely holding a bottle of water. The bottle was full. She took sips in time with the music playing through the speaker in the ceiling. One measure - 1 2 3 4 - to bring the rubber straw to her teeth. Two measures - 1 2 3 4 1 2 3 4 - to suck. One measure - 1 2 3 4 - to bring it back to its place between her legs, halfway up her thighs. Two measures - 1 2 3 4 - to rest. Repeat.

The girl in the black shorts ascended the stairs with the best posture imaginable. Her gaze was forward, her shoulders down, everything was in line. She spotted the girl in the green dress and the corners of her mouth peeked up into a peaceful smile. She walked toward her; the girl in the green dress stood up, wrapped her arms around the other's neck and pressed the bridge of her nose into her collarbone. The girl in the black shorts kept holding on to the girl's waist even as she started to pull away. The girl in the green dress was not smiling.

She started to speak, staring at the girl in the black shorts daringly, trying to challenge her. The girl in the black shorts kept that tranquil smile, she would not come undone. She spoke briefly, raised her eyebrows and cheeks, showing her teeth. The girl in the green dress shook her head, glanced at her phone. The girl in the black shorts looked at the phone, spoke again, looked at the other with raised eyebrows and quiet smile; and the girl in the green dress shook her head again, this time with force.

The phone lit up, the girl in the black shorts grabbed it and set it down on the table, at the same time placing the girl in the green dress' hand on her heart. One word was spoken. The girl in the green dress recoiled, picked up her phone and started to walk towards the stairs. The girl in the black shorts didn't follow, instead smiled to herself and bent down to the flower bed lining the stairs. She picked the smallest one, then another of the same, and another. Weeds. She tied one stem around another's petals, and again, and again, until a bracelet was made. The girl in the green dress paused at the bottom of the stairs to sip one more measure of water. The girl in the black shorts walked steadily toward the girl in the green dress, offered the floral friendship to her. The girl in the green dress slipped it over her wrist without really looking at it. The girl in the green dress was not smiling.

CONTENTLESS SCENE #2

A: I'm sorry.

B: I know.

A: I truly am sorry.

B: Stop.

A: Why?

B: You know what it does to me.

A: Yeah but I forget.

B: Try to not. Think on it.

A: Okay.

B: Thank you.

INK'S LAKE, TX

We heard the noise at about 9:18 pm. It was ear splitting, I actually reached up to my ear to make sure it wasn't ripping in half. It took probably 50 blows of the whistle before we figured we should look for the source. 50. That's almost a minute. Can't imagine how long that minute felt to that girl. We followed the metal shrieks, searching in the dark for something we weren't sure we wanted to find; not sure it was found once we came upon her. Her position was in a ball, shins on the ground, back flat, chin up, gazing forward, both hands on the whistle. She was still, her body paralyzed, all except for her mouth, ceaselessly blowing that whistle. Once we approached her, we thought she would stop. But she didn't stop. She blew and blew the whistle, staring at the bushes, or beyond. She didn't talk. We asked her if she was okay, we asked her if she could hear us, we asked her name. She didn't answer. I don't know how it would have helped, if she did answer.

But she kept on blowing
Keeping the rhythm
Excruciating as a siren
Helpless as a lamb.

PRESENT STUDY

SLIPPING THROUGH MY FINGERS

The tigress shows her face to me again today
I associate with the girl who wears no makeup and beads in her hair

I ask if she knows her
And she says No, probably not, not yet

I tell her how I am looking to reach this girl
I am shaking the phone trees, and wandering the plaza

I see the van at the farmers market
But she is nowhere to be found

MOMENT DU JOUR

Baker and oven repairer
Singing along, to themselves
To The Piano Man

BASEMENT LIFE

When the people above you seem worlds away
You only hear them when they're fighting or fucking
And every so often it sounds as if they are rolling a bowling ball
From one end of the house to another

Not fully underground, no
The bottom of the windows are level with the dirt

But

No one knocks on your door at Halloween

BOOK ON TAPE

I want to be the kind of person
That sends you audio recordings every day

Reading a book on meditation
Since I can't be at your bedside

But I'm the kind of person
That forgets to put on deodorant
Half the time

INSIDE, WITH THE DOOR OPEN

Today I can't tell if my upstairs neighbor is rearranging
Or if it is the thunder

Today my inkblots fall from the wall
And I have two teas, but one mug

Today I finally take out the trash bags under my eyes
But the mailman tells me Sorry, Hun, we don't recycle love potion

Today I have a double feature in my home theatre for three
And get engaged to the smoke rings in the air

THE WORKERS

Most of the people in the world who touch money all of the time
Don't have it

Aren't phased by handling it, yet never consider it held

Are disgusted by it

The people who see it daily in their hands never see it in their lives

Working for
What they work with

BLACK ROCK, TX

She sits alone in her tent
Atop layers and layers of blankets
Yet she can still feel the ground underneath
Her buttbones balance on two nubs of grass
As she pushes down and opens the bottle
I wonder, she thinks to herself
How many pills I can swallow at a time
Must add up from one, or it doesn't count
Let's make it a game

One; total-> one.
Two; total-> three.
Three; total-> six.
Four; total-> ten.
Five; total-> fifteen.

She sets down the thermos of cold water
Taking care to tighten the top closed
Before sliding to the earth
And staring at the stars
Finally, she says out loud
I've won

CENOTÉ

Those chairs give him such good posture; he shifts
We seem to scatter our dice up the wall; all of the 3's are upside down
And the wicker bicycle looks like a drag.
No wonder the fans on her eyelids are fake; she blinks

We're only open when lit up from the outside

WHO AM I #2

I am tiny mountains in the wall
I am someplace where all the people feel safe
I am a radiating sunset, the infinite rising and falling on the horizon
I am monster mouths and pulsing stars, orgasmic flowers and cell bars
And ripped paper pieces on the ground
What am I?

USED

My dishes
Are like children
I bathe them
I make them food
I watch them grow
From clean, smooth infants
To [tea-ring] stained, corner-chipped, grooved, cracked, spilled, spotted,
burnt, bruised, battered
Beauties

WHERE WAS YOUR BRAIN THIS MORNING, MISS?

Well that I simply don't know

I could say it was in the forest
Looking for a reason not to drown

I could say it was in the teabag
Searching for a way not to burn

I could say it was on the wall
Hoping the vines would teach it to coexist

I could say it was folded in the dictionary
Finding the definition of self-love

I could say it was in bed, paralyzed
But it will be lying

CONTENTLESS SCENE #3

A: I am not.

B: You sure?

A: You really think I am?

B: No. I know better.

A: I hope so.

B: I do. Sorry.

A: Don't be.

B: God, please come here.

THE SINGING WOMAN

A person pulls up to the red light on a motorcycle, and hears a woman singing through her open window. There is no one else on the vast, windy road at this time of night. The motorcyclist can't make out the words of the song through her helmet, only the rough, untrained sound of the woman's voice just slightly louder than the accompanying music. She dares not look directly at the singing woman, for her helmet is large and she would need to turn her whole head to see. Her engine revs as she turns her head to the right, at an angle, and lifts her eyes just so to find an unsteady reflection in the visor of her helmet. The singing woman is crying, she can see now. Another car pulls around the bend behind her and her view is temporarily blinded by headlights, she squints. Just as she is able to see plainly the face of the songstress once more, the light turns green; she hesitates to accelerate long enough to see her mouth one word: "Hallelujah".

The singing woman arrives at the shoddy-lit house in a trance. Each movement feels like a deja vu; the locking of the car, the walk through the yard. Stopping at the door of her partner's house, she shrugs her shoulders, releasing them pointedly, and staying relaxed. She need not be seen crying, since she barely knows the reason herself. The door opens with ease, and she proceeds inside with a steady breath. As she turns the corner at the end of the long wall of coats, she notices, behind them, a door. A door she has never remembered seeing before. Pausing to stare a moment longer, she can't get the music out of her head. The same four notes, intruding so much as to make her think she actually hears them. She carries on, resolving that it is just a weary creak in the artificial blueberry smelling, splitting wood floor.

ANALYSIS

APRIL 12TH

I feel so bad for the birds
Trying to make homes on these naked trees

Sometimes I feel like a naked tree
Trying to root in the gusts and storms
Wanting to be full and whole
Trying to give just a couple of creatures a home

NO, LOVE

You don't want to do this
Put the pins down
And go to bed
Sleeping will help

I know you like to be alone
But I'm here
And I have those thoughts, those urges, those preoccupations too
Be alone with me
Be asleep with me

WHO AM I? #3

I am a sandcastle in a bathtub
I am the object of envy
I am a goddess with the fate of a saber tooth
I am burdened but I am functioning
What am I?

HERBOLOGICAL HOME

Are there any plants that thrive
Being uprooted and re-sown elsewhere
Every few years?

CONTENTLESS SCENE #4

A: Goddamnit.

B: It's okay.

A: No, I fucked it up.

B: It's happened before.

A: It being fucked up or me fucking things up?

B: ....Both. No the first one.

A: Okay.

B: No. Both.

KNOW TO BE USEFUL, BELIEVE TO BE BEAUTIFUL

And then one morning
She sees all of her possessions
And adds up all of the weight in her head
And realizes she'd drown in it

If
                    it were all piled on top of her
                    it were water, all that water,
                    it and she were shoved into a space smaller than
                    its volume
What if
She picks up a
                    bag,
                    backpack,
                    picnic basket

What if she goes on that picnic
She'll need that basket

She realizes she shouldn't live by 'what if'

What if she finally makes that collage quilt
She knows she never will
She woke up and knew
The knowledge of the necessary

She sees a shoe
Notices she likes the cut but not the color
Remembers she likes other things for their function but not their aesthetic

Wonders if she likes people for the same reason

She finds a necklace
                    two necklaces
                    three necklaces
                    a ball of necklaces
She always liked untangling necklaces
No, that's not true
She was always good at untangling necklaces
She reminds herself
                    those are different things
                    to keep noticing when those things are different
                    and when they are separate

She gets rid of all of her
                    necklaces because those can tangle
                    shoelaces because those can tangle
                    scarves because those can tangle

She gets rid of all of her
                    wrapping ribbons because those can tangle
                    computer cords because those can tangle
                    eyelashes because those can tangle

She gets rid of all of her
                    strings of lights because those can tangle
                    bank accounts because those can tangle
                    hairs because those can tangle
She gets rid of all of her   relationships because those can tangle
She gets rid of all of her   veins because those can tangle

COMMUTER

Your life has been like a nighttime bike ride against the freezing wind:

Turn your head away and your ears are free
But then you see the shadows
Or pressure of light circles behind you
When you finally get off
Your legs are shaky, your chest is tight, and you can't breathe through your
mouth or your nose

Everything would have been different
If only the wind had been at your back.

FINDINGS

SOME PEOPLE

Some people don't

> question it
> like to be touched gently
> love themselves but don't do anything about it

Some people are

> scared of the sun
> addicted to some people

Some people aren't

> mysterious on purpose

Some people laugh when they're mad

Some people respond better to being informed in stages rather than all at once

Some people

> can't fall in love overnight
> drink coffee for the taste

Some people die when they want to

Some people have secrets

> they don't even know about

CONTENTLESS SCENE #5

A: Have you tried it?

B: No. Never before this.

A: Why not?

B: Dunno. So you have?

A: Yeah.

B: Do you regret it?

A: Sometimes.

B: Yeah.

A: Yeah.

SLICK

I'm not an idiot
I can lick a knife without hurting m-
Ow

WHO AM I? #4

I am two rolls of paper and a box of grass
I am penniless in estate and affection
I am pregnant with ideas, and
I am ashamed of my fickle, pickled heart
What am I?

FORM

I wish I was the inventor of the "emergency contact"
The subtle yet ceaseless acknowledgement that people *need* each other

I wonder how many emergency contacts are matched up, reciprocated

WAITING FOR THE BUS AT WALMART IN THE RAIN, THINKING ABOUT DEATH

Anything can kill you
There are very few things that can keep you alive

I can live without you

But I can't live without death
No one can

CRUISER

Friendship is like a bike that never rusts
It may gather cobwebs
But you brush them away with a wave of the hand
And it works just as well

WHO AM I #5

I am a tropical island precipice, adjacent the volcano
I am aching from the inside out
I am royal and I am high
I am wounded by the one that can heal me
What am I?

ADVICE TO A SELF-IDENTIFIED HERMIT

Leave the house every once in a while
If just to determine, upon your return
The presence of an odor

CONTENTLESS SCENE #6

A: It's fucking useless.

B: I'm sorry.

A: Between that and relationships I'm done.

B: I'm falling asleep but I don't want to stop talking to you.

A: It's late. Go to sleep.

B: I want you to be safe.

A: Ok.

B: Goodnight.

A: Night.

NOT A CONFESSION

If the plane were going down
I have no one to call and confess my love to
And even if I did
My instinct would be to call my parents

And go out like I came in
With them

CONCLUSION

MOVING FORWARD

Four women in a carriage
Hanging over the edge and sitting patiently on crushed velvet
Watching the geometrical metal and watching each other

Two women on a puzzle
Racing the sunset and racing the fire-ants
Hearing cat-calls and coyote cries

One woman on a rocking chair
Looking through cobwebs and symmetrical bars
Seeing through flashy, glowy, gay lights
Peering through bubbles, and screws, and hairs
At all the people
Embracing

THE 1%

The richest thing in the world is
Death
Death gets everything
In the end

CONTENTLESS SCENE #7

A: I just-I just think you're really hot.

B: Well I think you're hot.

A: We're stupid.

B: I know.

A: I love you.

B: I love you.

LIVING PROJECT

I have a box of fabric
Of greens and purples and blue
I have a box of fabric
That I would share with you
I have a box of fabric
For when I want to split in two
Instead I split the fabric
And make a scrap a new

I have a box of fabric
Of blues and purples and green
I have a box of fabric
That you may not have seen
I have a box of fabric
For when I'm feeling mean
Instead I'm mean to scrappy fabric
Insisting cuts be clean

I have a box of fabric
That I'm making into flags
I have a box of fabric
For when my soul sags
I have a box of fabric
For when I want to cut
Instead I cut the fabric
Singing prayers from my gut

I have a box of fabric
Of purples and greens and red

I have a box of fabric
A reminder for my head
I have a box of fabric
For when I want to shred
Instead I shred red fabric
The prayers, the reason I'm not dead

I have a box of fabric
Becoming flags of prayer
I have a box of fabric
That will soon be in the air
I have a box of fabric
That I will gladly share
I have a box of fabric
A box of self-care

PEDESTRIAN

The sound and smell
Of finally dry tires
On finally dry ground
Coming to a halt
For you

BECAUSE # 2

Because I apologized to the banana as I put it in the smoothie
"I'm sorry you're so bruised"
That banana wasn't sorry, it said
"You're using me!
That is my purpose
Now you will be healthy and live longer, better
So others can use you!"

EVOLUTION

Everything is a creation
    The universe's creation
        The universe's creations' creation
            The universe's creations' creation's creation
Create every day
    Create something
    And show no one
        Create something
        And show everyone
Create lots of teensy things
        Create one great big thing
Create a few teensy things and a handful of larger things
Create a language
    A code
        A map
            For yourself
                Create a lie detector
                    An alarm clock
                        A compass
                            For your soul

                          Create a constitution
                        A bible
                A dictionary
            For yourself
           Create a thermometer
        A calculator
    A periscope
For your soul

WHO AM I? #6

I am a psychological scab picker
I am an atrium with an autographic memory
I am hopeful that I will find hope
I am accessible and unattainable
And I have come full circle
What am I?

ON THE WAY HOME

The time has come to pick up the toppled house plants,
And clean the cobwebs from between our toes.
To see through unfocused iris
At all the blue, that beautiful blue.

The time has come to get over the ghost.
To thank the sun for blowing and the wind for shining,
And fall in love with the sound of expanding
In our nostrils, chest and diaphragm.

The time has come to bleed out the unfeeling,
And yield to the commandeering
Of our mental methodology.
To take refuge in us, we, and it.

The time has come to recover the slices of our mind from the bottom.
Bow to them, let them respirate.
To ignite the pilot light of our gut.
To shake the hand that broke our heart.

Where has our mind been dwelling?

POEMS ARE CONFESSIONS

Forgive me world, for I have lived
I've felt and been felt
I've thought about death and cared about life
I've eaten and fucked and loved at the wrong times
And I regret nothing

What gets me is, there *is* enough...

OTHER WORKS BY THE AUTHOR

The Cessation Of Love

Felt Like Forever (a two-act play)

RAW; Poetry and Prose for the Queer, Sentient Being

Special Thanks to anyone who has ever given me a ride home; to the job doers that do the jobs no one thinks about; to those that voice love from the hilltops and windowsills and sidewalks; to my, and all teachers; to the non-violent protestors of violence; to the dancers and the chefs and the authors; to every single human that has ever had music be a product of their energies; to the farmers; to the fuckers; to the forgivers; and even, to the forgetters.

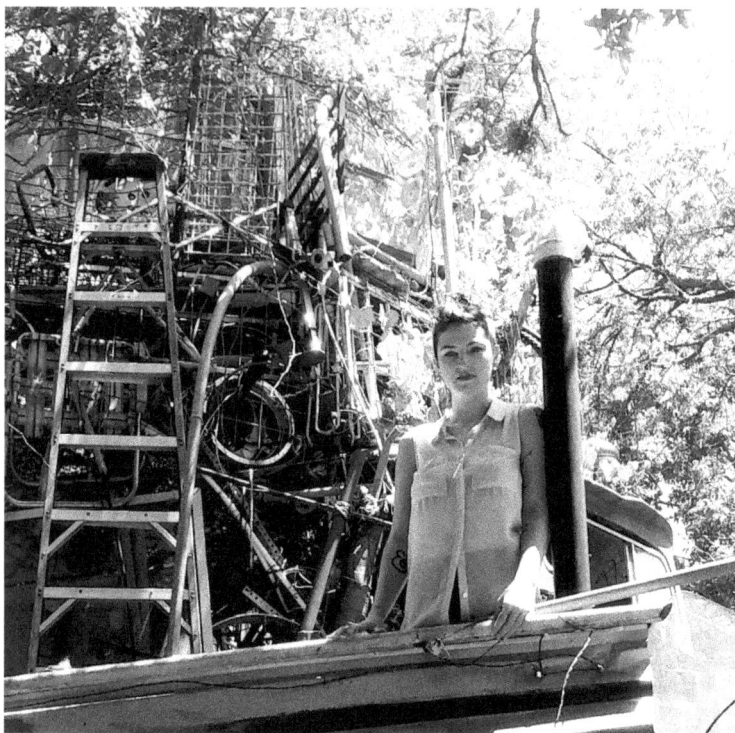

In addition to poetry, RAW writes for the theatre: with one completed full-length, and a compilation of short plays in the works. She toys with photography, is a part-time figure drawing model, and performs burlesque dance under the name Rebel Raspberry. A femme lesbian, queerity is at the root of all her work, intending to expose and re-envision a culture for gender & sexual minorities.

Rachel and her cat, Garcia, live in a fairytale flat in Austin, where she is a pastry chef, currently learning the craft of croissants.